The Vocal and Music Artistry

Companion Sheet Music

Cast Your Net Again…
For Such a Time as This

LANA LEE MARLER

ARCHWAY
PUBLISHING

Archway Publishing books may be ordered through booksellers or by contacting:

Archway Publishing
1663 Liberty Drive
Bloomington, IN 47403
www.archwaypublishing.com
844-669-3957

Because of the dynamic nature of the Internet, any web addresses or links contained in this book may have changed since publication and may no longer be valid. The views expressed in this work are solely those of the author and do not necessarily reflect the views of the publisher, and the publisher hereby disclaims any responsibility for them.

Any people depicted in stock imagery provided by Getty Images are models, and such images are being used for illustrative purposes only. Certain stock imagery © Getty Images.

ISBN: 978-1-6657-1885-1 (sc)
ISBN: 978-1-6657-1886-8 (e)

Library of Congress Control Number: 2022903008

Print information available on the last page.

Archway Publishing rev. date: 03/29/2022

Contents

*These songs were written with additional instruments. The full scores to these pieces are available upon request by contacting Lana Lee Marler directly at lwmarler@aol.com

Amazing Grace

Lyrics by John Newton
Music: New Britain
Arrangement by Basil Alter

6

Amazing Grace

come _____ Tis ___ grace has __ brought me __ safe thus

far And grace will lead me home. When

Verse 4

we've been there ten __ thou - sand years Bright, shi - ning as the __

Amazing Grace

sun _____ We've ____ no less ____ days to ____ sing God's

praise _____ Than ____ when we've first be - gun.

rit.

very slow roll, ad lib

A Quiet Room

Lyrics by Leslie Weatherhead
Music by Lana Lee Marler
Arrangement by Jeremy Johnson

A Quiet Room

12

A Quiet Room

There is No I in You

Lyrics and Music by Lana Lee Marler
Arrangement by Jeremy Johnson

14

There is No I in You

Chorus

sheep. Eyes close to the si - lent___ rhy - thm of each breath so ser - ene - ly gi - v'n.___ There is no I in You. All that I have, I re - cieve. You a - lone___ are

There is No I in You

There is No I in You

There is No I in You

Verse 3

is no I in You, Death's dark dream shall not pre - vail; the walk - ing

song of ___ all is ___ that your love ne - ver

Chorus

fails. ___ There is no I in You. All that I have I re -

There is No I in You

Just

Lyrics by unknown author and Lana Lee Marler
Music by Lana Lee Marler
Arrangement by Basil Alter

Just

Just

Just

From Love... To Love

Lyrics and Music by Lana Lee Marler
Arrangement by Basil Alter

Ho - ly __ Sav - ior, the An - gel brings good news to all both heav'n and

From Love... To Love

bur - den all for us. Come in our hearts blest Vir - gin's Son, re -

deemed by grace, the vic - 'try won. Your love, O God, pur - sues us still; grant that

we may do your will.

From Love... To Love

28

From Love... To Love

His Face

Lyrics by Helen H. Lemmel and Lana Lee Marler
Music by Lana Lee Marler
Arrangement by Basil Alter

O__ my soul I am so we-ary and trou-bled; There is no light in__ the

His Face

His Face

Light of His glo - ry ____ and grace.

His ____ word shall not fail me, He pro - mised; Be - lieve Him ____ and

all shall ____ be well. Then I will go to ____ a world that is dy - ing,

sim.

His Face

His Face

grace.

I feel so ver - y

thank - ful; it makes my heart sing. ____ New life I have been

His Face

giv - en By the Mak - er of all things. I find it hard to fath - om; it's won - der - ful to know;____ My sins are all for - giv - en as I look on Je - sus'

His Face

Jesus Said

Lyrics from New Testament Gospels Matthew and John
Adapted by Lana Lee Marler
Music by Lana Lee Marler
Arrangement by Robert Totten

Jesus Said

Jesus Said

The first and grea-test com-mand-ment___ is

love the Lord___ your God with all your___

heart, soul,___ mind and___ strength.___ The

Jesus Said

Jesus Said

Jesus Said

Jesus Said

By this ____ shall men know ____ you are ____ my dis - ci - ples ____ if you ____ have love one ____ for a -

Jesus Said

Prayer of the Goat

Lyrics adapted by Lana Lee Marler
from poem by Carmen Benos de Gasztold
Music: Ebenezer Tune composed by Thomas John Williams
Arrangement by Basil Alter

Prayer of the Goat

Prayer of the Goat

Prayer of the Goat

Lord the sheep do not un-der stand. They graze and graze, all

in the same di-rec-tion. Lord, let me live as an ad - ven-tur-er,

quiv - 'ring with de - light on the sum - mit of the world!

Amazing Love.. How Can It Be?

Lyrics by Charles Wesley
Adapted Lyrics and Music by Lana Marler
Arrangement by Basil Alter

Amazing Love.. How Can It Be?

help - less __ race.   A - ma-zing love! How

can __ it __ be __ That Thou, my God should die __ for __ me?

Died He for me, who caused His pain. __ For me, who Him to death __ pur -

O Holy Vision Most Glorious

Lyrics and Music by Lana Lee Marler
Arrangement by Basil Alter

O Holy Vision Most Glorious

55

O Holy Vision Most Glorious

spi - rit is quick - ened as well. Things too mar - vel - ous are

gi - f - ting, the ho - ri - zon re - veal - ing its tell.

O ho - ly vi - sion most glo - ri - ous, at

O Holy Vision Most Glorious

last our eyes' long - ing be - hold. The shimm-ering of God's hope

for us, as the gold streets of Hea - ven un - fold.

The

O Holy Vision Most Glorious

O Holy Vision Most Glorious

Swept in-to light ev-er-las——ting, the ques - tions of life, there are

none.—— Our God, who-se breath is all gi - ving, calls

us to where all breaths are one.——

O Holy Vision Most Glorious

O Holy Vision Most Glorious

As the gold streets of hea - ven un -

fold.

References

Bonnell, Daniel, 2021. *Cast Your Net,* used by permission of Bonnell, Daniel, 2021, Front Book Cover Art

Newton, J., 1779., Britain, New, Alter, Basil, 2021 *Amazing Grace - Wikipedia.* [online] En.wikipedia. org. Available at: <https://en.wikipedia.org/wiki/Amazing_Grace>, public domain p. 5

A Quiet Room Etchells, R., 2008. *Just as I am.* London: SPCK, p.62-63, Weatherhead, L., 1985. *A Private House of Prayer.* New York: Abingdon Press, p.176, Marler, L. and Johnson, Jeremy, 2021, used by permission of Marler, L. and Johnson, Jeremy, 2021, p. 10

Marler, L. and Johnson, Jeremy, 2021. *There is No I in You,* used by permission of Marler, L. and Johnson, Jeremy, 2021, p. 13

Unknown, Marler, L., Alter, Basil, 2021. *Just,* used by permission of Marler, L. and Alter, Basil, 2021, p. 20

Marler, L. and Alter, Basil, 2021. *From Love … To Love,* used by permission of Marler, L. and Alter, Basil, 2021, p. 24

Lemmel, H., 1922, *Turn Your Eyes Upon Jesus.* [online] Hymnary.org. Available at: <https://hymnary. org/text/o_soul_are_you_weary_and_troubled>, Marler, L. and Alter, Basil, *His Face,* used by permission of Marler, L. and Alter, Basil, 2021, p. 29

Gospels of Matthew and John, New Testament, Marler, L., and Totten, Robert, 2021, *Jesus Said,* used by permission of Marler, L. and Totten, Robert, 2021 p. 36

Gasztold, C., Godden, R. and Primrose, J., 1947 *Prayers From the Ark.* Gasztold, C. and Etchells, R., 2008. *Just as I am.* London: SPCK, p.50. Marler, L., Williams, J. Thomas, and Alter, Basil, 2021. *Prayer of the Goat.* Memphis, used by permission of Marler, L. and Alter, Basil, 2021 p. 44

Wesley, C., 1738. *And Can It Be, That I Should Gain?* [online] [public domain] Hymnary.org. Available at: <https://hymnary.org/text/and_can_it_be_that_i_should_gain> Marler, L. and Alter, Basil, 2021. *Amazing Love...How Can It Be.* Memphis, used by permission of Marler, L. and Alter, Basil, 2021, p. 48

Marler, L. and Alter, Basil, 2021. *O Holy Vision Most Glorious,* used by permission of Marler, L. and Alter, Basil, 2021, p. 53

Hamilton, Julie, 2021. *Stairway to Heaven* used by permission of Hamilton, Julie, 2021, Back Book Cover Art

Printed in the United States
by Baker & Taylor Publisher Services